POEMS

&

SONGS

Irene (Shaloma) Levi

is peace in Greek,
Shalom: Hebrew

ISBN 978-965-7542-11-8

Contact Information
Email: ilevi@013.net
P.O.Box 7438,
Jerusalem 91071, Israel.

Published by Tsur Tsina Publications
Lay-out and graphic design: Petra van der Zande

ORDER INFORMATION

1. http://www.Lulu.com
2. Via Irene personally
3. Write to email: tsurtsinapublications@gmail.com

THIS BOOK IS PUBLISHED

IN HONOUR OF MY

93rd BIRTHDAY in 2012

A Present From my Dear Friend Petra

CONTENTS

CONTENTS

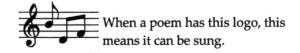

When a poem has this logo, this means it can be sung.

From McComb to Jerusalem chronicles my life from the time I was born in McComb, Ohio, USA, to the way God led me to live in Jerusalem, *haMakome* (The Place), Israel. The book is written by Petra van der Zande.

ORDER INFORMATION

1. http://www.Lulu.com
2. Via Irene personally
3. Write to email: tsurtsinapublications@gmail.com

THE WORDLESS BOOK
(adapted to the original)

M y heart was black with sin   **_BLACK_**
Until the Savior came in
His precious Blood I know   **_RED_**
Has washed me whiter than snow   **_WHITE_**

CHORUS:
Oh wonderful, wonderful way
To walk with Jesus each day.

He showers His gifts from above   **_BLUE_**
And helps me grow in His Love   **_GREEN_**
I want the world each to see
He'd save the worst - He saved me!

CHORUS

In Heaven's gold streets then we'll sing   **_GOLD_**
Forever to our Great King!

THANK YOU, LORD

How could you be so true
To one so unlike You?
I cannot understand this, Lord!
Such mercies can they be to sinners, even me.
Thy grace has overwhelmed me, Lord,

CHORUS
I never can repay, But from my heart I say:
Oh thank You, thank You, thank You, Lord.
My heart, my lips my mind
The words just cannot find,
To tell You how I thank You, Lord.

You grant my each request
With extras I am blessed,
I cannot understand this, Lord,
My hands, my ears, my eyes
You thrill with each surprise.
Thy grace has overwhelmed me, Lord.

CHORUS

Such love, and oh, such grace
To die there in my place.
Oh, teach me all this Truth, dear Lord,
And now life's best with You
Is crowned with Heaven too
There, with all saints we'll praise You, Lord.

MESSIAH

M̶ashiach, Massiach, Messiah ~ He's One,
The **Anointed**: the King, Prophet, Priest, perfect Son.
Yeshua, Yessua - mankind's **Savior's** come forth,
Last Adam, through His blood!
Brings new life on earth!

Call to Israel

*I*t is finished!" Jesus cried -
Calvary's Emancipator!
And in my heart that echo rang
Two thousand long years later.

In Adam's race I too had sinned
And God seemed far way
Until His spirit wooed and won
To Calvary's Lamb that day.

My baptism service

"I'm saved!" Oh, hallelujah!"
Forever I'll dwell with Thee.
My sins forgiven, my Home in Heaven,
And Thy Spirit dwells in me!

The Way I'd found, as student,
The Truth, as glad school teacher,
The Life, in homes, in Bible groups,
For Christ a ready preacher.

And then, God showed me Israel,
And shared with me His tears
For these, His chosen people
So blinded through the years.

"Will you share with them My mercy
And Love them to Messiah?
Salvation came through Jews to you,
Can you their Own deny them?"

1948, on the ship to-
ward Israel, via Leba-
non, holding my Bible.

"Oh, take from me, Lord Jesus,
If need be, all my bliss
I've found in Thee, if in my place
Thy people could find this."

And so, with Him,
I've reached out
And found Jews everywhere.
I've opened to them His treasure
And prayed, "Lord, let them
share!"

Bibles, ready for distribution

Took for schools, etc,   11

In prophetic Word unfolding
To their homeland they're returning
There, too, He led in my life's plan
To share Christ, with deep yearning.

New immigrant camp in Israel

He's coming back, be ready!
Israel, Behold thy King!
God of His Word lives, see, oh earth!
True Christians, rise and sing!

Performance of Händel's *Messiah* from 1960 onward throughout Israel. Today, it is also sung in Hebrew.

12

The Story Behind the Four Poems

$\mathcal{I}$n 1947, I moved to New York's Lower East Side. On the first morning, I woke up with the following titles: **"Rahab's Grace"**; **"Rebecca's Gems"**; **"Rachel's Glory"** and **"Ruth's Gleanings"**. Describing my calling, the words began to come forth.

****

The names of four women relate to my physical roots. My mother's name was **OLIVE** - a tree which brings forth 'olive oil for anointing'. Through the 'good olive tree' (Romans 11:24) ~ I am grafted into the God of Israel. And how much more Israel!

GRACE (one of my mother's sisters): the story of my life when I saw His Amazing Grace in forgiveness and new life in Christ. **RUTH** and **NAOMI** (also mom's sisters): each were much a part of my life.

RAHAB'S GRACE

Joshua ~ type of Jesus as Deliverer ~ Joshua 2:6
Rahab ~ type of Gentile believers

They were considered spies,
Though the land belonged to them,
When Joshua came to Canaan,
To bring Israel in again.

Rahab showed them mercy,
Harlot though she be
She sheltered them within her house
Lest Satan's hosts should see.

She recognized the Jews' One God,
The Lord of all creation,
Was still the Mighty One to save
Her with the Jewish nation.

By a cord they made escape
Through this Gentile's window.
"Wilt thou be hid for three sad days?
To the Mountain thou shalt then go."

"This scarlet cord which saved us Jews
From the pursuer's face,
When thou shalt in thy window bind,
'Twill save you by our grace."

So Joshua saved this Rahab
And Joshua saved the Jews
Whenever God saves anyone
The scarlet line He'll use.

Jesus is "Yoshua" – Savior
Leads out of sin to His Land
The scarlet line - His precious Blood,
Written with God's own Hand....

Hang it in your life's window.
To save God's "spies" and you
When the Trumpet
sounds
and this world falls,
Christ takes His saved
ones through.

REBECCA'S GEMS

Isaac ~ type of Christ the Son, seeking a Bride ~ believers ~
through the Holy Spirit. Genesis 24

I am the Father's servant,
You are kind to give me to eat,
But first I must tell you my errand
To make this journey complete.

My Master is wondrously wealthy,
And he has an only Son.
To Him He has given all things,
And unto His chosen one.

You are the one He has chosen
To become His bride today.
Are you willing to leave all and follow,
To meet Him at the end of the way?

My Master said, "Go to My kindred;
The angel shall prosper thee there.
If the called one be not willing to follow,
Thou art free; but this time my Son spare."

Behold these gems and this raiment,
The Son has riches untold!
There is nothing His bride shall be wanting,
And His love is a jewel of gold.

Oh, Rebekah, don't keep Him waiting;
He longs to own you right now
Thy family will give you their blessing
As they see how blessed **art** thou.

And oh, the journey's not tiresome,
You'll soon see the One you adore.
You'll 'light off your camel' to meet Him
While He greets you as His evermore!

EVEN SO, COME QUICKLY, LORD JESUS!

RACHEL'S GLORY

Joseph ~ type of Christ as Beloved Son and forgiving Brother;
rejected, then exalted. Genesis 37-50

*R*achel's one main glory
Was hidden in her son;
Of all of Israel's children,
He was the chosen one.

The other sons of Jacob
Were jealous of Joseph's state
They sold him into Egypt
Thus to vent their hate.

Later Joseph fed them
When they came down for corn.
How he longed to enlighten, forgive them
And again with his family be one.

In fullness of time, in his glory
Yet his heart running over with tears,
He revealed himself to his brethren
And his life and love through all those years.

So Rachel had one chief glory,
Like Mary, the Lord Jesus' mother.
My one main glory ~ to show Israel's seed
Their Savior, Christ Jesus ~ **their Brother!**

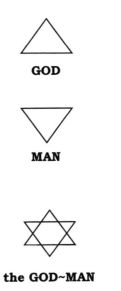

GOD

MAN

the GOD~MAN

Messiah ~ Christ
Coming soon to reign

David's Shield (*Magen David*) and mine ~
He took the darts that were meant for me!

RUTH'S GLEANINGS

Boaz ~ type of Christ as Kinsman Redeemer.
Ruth ~ Gentile believers ~ grafted in

I'm just a Gentile believer,
I've come to the God of the Jews,
Forsaken my old life in "exile"
To live where my God shall choose.

I hear that you Jews love strangers,
That you let them glean in your fields;
Already you're dropped handfuls on purpose
And I've had such bounteous yields.

Such gleanings from sacred pages
The Jews have let fall for me:
These sheaves from which I'm now gleaning
Are all so fruitful and free!

Why, O Naomi's Kinsman,
Shouldst thou take knowledge of me
Seeing I am a stranger,
And not of Israel like thee?

A full reward Thou hast given,
O Lord God of Israel!
As under Thy wings I'm now trusting,
Here all's so abundantly well.

At last I am one with Thy people
Through Thee Who alone couldst redeem,
O Israel's great Kinsman, my Bridegroom,
Forever together we'll glean!

SONG of BOAZ and RUTH

Hearest thou not, my daughter
Go not to glean elsewhere
Here in my field at 'House of Bread'
You'll find all you need, I swear.

Oh, my Lord, oh, my Lord,
I fall on my face to thee
Why should I find with thee such grace
That thou takest thought for me?

It has been fully shown me
How thou hast left thy land,
Joining a people you knew not
You've clung to Naomi's hand.

Oh, my lord, oh, my lord,
What comfort to me you've shown.
That thou hast spoken friendly thus
Though I be not like thine own.

A full reward be given thee,
Thy work find recompense
In the Lord God of Israel!
There's under these wings defense.

Oh, Boaz, thou my strength
Thy grace overpowers my heart
Nowhere on earth would safety be
If I were from thee apart.

At mealtime come thou hither
Here with my reapers dine
Glean from my sheaves and all that falls,
Partake of my bread and wine.

Oh, my Lord,
oh, my Lord,
I've gleaned
and I'm so
sufficed
All of thy
riches, now
made mine,
Thou
Bridegroom -
Redeemer,
Christ.

The Story of Ruth
The Meaning of the Names

I'll not go back, I must go on;
I'll follow, follow on!
Thy God, **Naomi**, shall be mine,
Though all my kin be gone.
Though **Orpah** wants her safe, past base,
And turns her **back** to Israel's grace,
I, **Ruth**, must leave it all, from darkness into dawn.

My name means '**friendship**';
What price I pay for this.
To bear that curse of Moab,
As I enter Israel's bliss.
To share in Israel's God and good
No Moabitess ever could.
Yet entreat me not to leave you, Naomi, thee I kiss.

You call yourself now '**Mara**' - how **bitter** exile's sting;
Yet still your God is faithful back to your land to bring.
I'll help to change this bitter state,
And **pleasant** then will be your fate.
Your last days shall be best of all, and then your heart will
sing!

The **Boaz** whom your people have given to crown my days
'In Him is strength',
Acceptance into Israel's heritage.
He's made me His and He is mine;
What union and new life divine!
They're yours, they're mine, in Israel's God,
To bring Messiah's praise.

Harvest at Bethlehem - over 100 years ago

RUTH'S STORY IN PICTURES

Valentine (Val) Vester's family had been part of the American Colony, a Christian community established in Eastern Jerusalem in 1881. Val and Dola Ben Yehuda's family had been friends, but during the nineteen years that Jerusalem was divided, they had been unable to visit each other. When the city was reunited in 1967, I had the joy of often driving the two women to each other's homes, so that they could visit each other. They looked at photo albums and exchanged books about their parents' lives – *Our Jerusalem,* the story of Val Vester's family (the Spaffords) and *Tongue of the Prophets,* about the life of Ben Yehuda. Spafford was the author of the famous song 'It is Well With my Soul'. (See page 166 *From McComb to Jerusalem).*

The "Ruth" in the following pictures was probably a young member of the American Colony community; the remaining "cast" were villagers from the Bethlehem area who were actually harvesting, threshing and winnowing their crops. These pictures were taken over 100 years ago.

Valentine (Val) Vester (left)
and Dola Wittman-Ben Yehuda (right).
Both holding each other's father's stories.

26

Ruth said, "Do not entreat me to leave you, to return from following you, for wherever you go, I will go... Your people shall be my people, your God my God."

And Naomi and Ruth both went on until they arrived at Bethlehem.

Ruth came to a field that belonged to Boaz who was of the family of Naomi's deceased husband. Boaz said to his servant, who stood over the reapers, "To whom does this maiden belong?"

27

Boaz said to Ruth, "Do not go to glean in another field... here you shall stay with my maidens."

Boaz said to her at mealtime, "Come here and partake of the bread..."
He ordered his servants "Pretend to forget some of the bundles for her."

Ruth carried it to the city and Naomi saw what she had gleaned.

Ruth came to the threshing floor and Boaz said, "Ready the shawl you are wearing and hold it," and she held it, and he measured out six measures of barley....

GOD'S HADASSAH

Oh Esther, God's Hadassah,
What treasured Truth is shown
God and His people hidden
Until His time be known.

Naught but a **living** Savior
Could foil that Haman's plot
To destroy God's chosen people!
The outcome - based on what?

The 'death' that came through fasting
Of three days in deep gloom,
The threat of death upon them
Like being in a tomb.

Then, 'risen', her bold decision
Though perish, and death face
Before the king and justice
Yet, lo! His scepter's grace.

'Twas salvation - end of story
Based on that 'death'-like fast
Our doom deserved, but life preserved
Our faith, God's work - at last.

About Stanley Duce

Stanley Joseph Duce, (often called Yusif) was a Bible teacher to the Middle East. We first met in the USA, and later again in Beirut, Lebanon, while on our way to Jerusalem, Israel. We married in December 1948 in Jerusalem and had our honeymoon in the Garden Tomb, in a cottage we called our 'Resurrection Residence'.

While I was the principal of the Carmel School, Stanley made several mission trips around the world.
He preached widely in several languages and wrote many articles, poems and letters, always glorifying the Lord. God called him Home in 1968.

ONE GOD

Our one Savior-Shepherd, one God ('tis not gold!)
In seeking lost sheep brings us back to one fold.
He said we are one, yet He prayed for this too.
Oh, Lord, that Your bought-ones belonged to just YOU!

There's only one Body, its members are we,
One Head whom we'll follow 'gainst one enemy.
With perfect design He directs all His own;
Through our love and harmony He shall be known.

There's only one Temple, and we're each a stone,
One Loaf to feed men, 'twas one Lamp whose Light shone;
Our High Priest is one, and all we are His priests,
From one Holy Scriptures we dine at His feasts.

Thy blest Holy Spirit stamps us with Your Name.
Your Breath formed one Adam,
Your Church knew one Flame -
One Fire, Lamb, and altar;
One Cloud, camp and land,
One nation, one King, 'tis one Captain's command.

One Way and one Truth,
One new Life, 'one accord',
One Faith and one Baptism, Power and Lord.
One Sun, from God's laws, and grace, shines on this earth;
One Son, God's and Adam's, through Whom we've new birth.

One Source of all help, quite enough for us all;
One Heart that is open to all who will call.
His wisdom apportions His gifts, works, and tests,
What Sabbath! Eternal and temporal rests!

One Bridegroom returns for His one prepared Bride
To take to one Heaven, to jointly abide.
On earth as in Heaven, Lord, help us to be
Rejoicing and serving as one Family!

Believers Bethesda Fellowship in Haifa, 1960's.
Stanley Duce in circle.

The Story Behind the Following Songs

From 1960-1967, I was invited to be the principal of the *Carmel* school in Haifa. This was a Bible-based school for Israeli children who lived in *Bethel*, a kind of boarding/foster home. The regular morning curriculum was taught in Hebrew, while in the afternoon, English lessons were given. I wrote the English and Hebrew words and the music for these two songs. The pupils sang these 'Alma Mater' songs in Hebrew, often while we were away on trips throughout Israel. 'Carmel' means: Vineyard of God. God's fire of Truth fell on Mt. Carmel. (Our school was located on Vine Street in Haifa). 'Bethel' means: House of God.

"Jerusalem of Gold" after the 1967 Six Day War. The Israeli flag proudly displayed at our school entrance.

34

BETHEL SONG

*D*ear home, dear mem'ry's stone, my Bethel,
It seems, my dreams, bring back so well,
God's ladder with his angels, I saw there, still I see,
And each one brings me nearer, O Jacob's God, to Thee;
For He, Christ Jesus, is God's Ladder
From earth to dwell in heaven, Beit El!

[We, his 'messengers' ministering upstairs and down there.]

CARMEL SCHOOL SONG

*H*ow sweet to eat your fruit, dear Carmel
God's vine is mine, in Him I dwell.
On Carmel fell God's fire,
Elijah's God still lives,
My heart he does inspire
And oh, what truth He gives,
For He, Christ Jesus, is God's altar,
His fire, His truth, His fruit – *Kerem-El.*

Poet E.A. Poe and Irene (née Poe) Levi

(My Physical Heritage)

*T*o many I'm known through the poet,
The world's heard of Poe, who's my kin.
But to God I am known by my Savior
I'm born into Christ, born again!

Poe may have evoked kindred feelings,
But did he convey Calv'ry's Truth?
One's personal relation to Jesus
Is God's measure of wisdom, forsooth!

The **raven** left the ark "Noah*-rest",
The **dove**, olive leaf, in "new earth" blest,
"No balm in Gilead?" Quote the **raven***, "No, Never!"
But the **Dove** on Christ's head - Balm forever!

* 'Noah' means rest ; Poe: "The Raven"; See Matthew 3:16-17; 9:12-13

Ben Yehuda and Hebrew

*B*en Yehuda's now known, reviving God's Truth,
In Hebrew, pure source, where all dig in its roots,
Knowing God better, but also His ways:
Bringing Jews home, **Hebrew lived**, in **our** days!

This is part of my spiritual heritage, made so real through my connection with the Ben Yehuda family.

I met Ada Reem (Ben Yehuda's daughter) while Wurmbrand spoke at the Finnish School in Jerusalem.

She and I bonded instantly because of our love for the Hebrew language. For many years, I rented a room in her apartment on King George Street, and got to know the extended Ben Yehuda family very well.

Dola and Ada, on the street named after their father - Eliezer Ben Yehuda.

"Irene and I are like Naomi and Ruth," Ada often joked.
In my book "From McComb to Jerusalem" are many stories about my involvement with the Ben Yehuda family.

CHANUKAH & CHRISTMAS

A great miracle was here"
At Chanukah, we say each year.
What miracle Messiah's birth
Who, by a virgin, came to earth.

(Isaiah 7:14)

Feasts of lights: eight lights relate
How oil for one night burned for eight.
The Light to Gentiles, with Israel,
Shines forth - His Name, "Emmanuel".

(Isaiah 42:6)

Enemies ruled in the land
Until arose that mighty band.
"The Mighty God", a Son, was given
To save from Satan unto Heaven.

(Isaiah 9:6)

In the temple, at this feast,
Jesus walked where Maccabees
Dedicated the house of stone.
He's **the** Temple, built by God alone.

(John 10:22)

Hasmoneans the altar cleansed
To worship God the way He'd planned.
Jesus cleansed the altar twice,
Became our Altar-Sacrifice.

(Isaiah 53)

I'm now His miracle, temple, light,
A pure and living sacrifice.
With those of old, we'll conquerors be,
With God, 'gainst one enemy.

OUR BROTHER - MESSIAH

A Dreamer of dreams to many He seems,
As He, o'er His brothers, grieves.
His stripes and His cloak to envy provoke.
To Him, must they bow their sheaves?

The Father at Home, for His sons as they roam,
Behold how His loving heart yearns.
He sends forth His Son, His own chosen One,
The stripes in that cloak He earns.

His cloak dipped in Blood, to the pit and then sold,
He, pieces of silver won;
To Gentiles, the world, and prison was hurled.
'Death' swallowed Life's purest Son.

But down in the depths God spoke to this death
And out of its sea He was cast;
Interpreting dreams of slaves and of kings
To honor and fame at last.

All ye who would live unto this One give
Thine homage, and take thy food.
His brothers, come see what Ruler is He,
Who makes you such feasts and good.

This brother of thine, of all of mankind,
He weeps as he sees you repent
"Behold Who I am, God's Son and God's Lamb
For LIFE I before was sent."

The Story Behind the Poem

(Excerpt from the book *From McComb to Jerusalem*, page 141)

It was the year 1969. The War of Attrition between Egypt and Israel wasn't over yet. A new song in Israel, *Balada Lachovesh*, was a ballad of a medic who gave his life while rescuing a wounded soldier. When the soldier realizes that he is alive, but the medic is dead, he cries out, ""*Ahi, ahi sheli!*", "My brother, oh, my brother!"

The song illustrated God's truth so well that I placed an open Hebrew Bible in the window of the Bible Bookshop on Agron street, showing Isaiah 61: "The Spirit anointed Me [Messiah] to 'bind up' the wounded." The Hebrew word for heal or bind up is the root of *Chovesh* - 'medic' in modern Hebrew. Messiah was the *Chovesh* who gave His life so that we could live – He truly was "Israel's Brother".

Balada Lachovesh could be heard everywhere you went – in the shops, on the street, from radios or people singing loudly *"Ahi, ahi sheli!"*

Many times I drove people to and from the airport. The evening that the song was aired for the first time, I was on my way back to Jerusalem, driving all alone. A new song came to me with a theme similar to Israel's 'Brother' song. I often handed out Elhanan Ben-Avraham's booklet about Joseph and his brothers. "This Brother of thine, of all mankind… Behold, Who I am, God's Son and God's Lamb…"

I realized anew that the same Spirit who works in individual believers also works in Israel as a nation. In the same way God often works in Israel and in the true Biblical Church, who are both chosen.

41

GOD'S SHEKINAH

$\mathcal{G}$od's *"Shekinah"*, on every *Shekhuna* (area)
to bless our *shekhaneem* (neighbors)
God's real *Mishkan* (Tabernacle) is seen.
One temple here, God's Presence very near
Thou Prince of Peace appear in Israel.

The Word became flesh and *shakhan* [dwells] among us.

Meeting friends in the garden outside my apartment.

J. believers

WEDDING POEM

Oh, Father, Your Love has changed our hearts well
Mine, and my Eliyah's, and through us - Israel.
We'd be Your true "Levites" and share Your blest way
Praying, believing, till that glorious day.

When we'll lay at Your feet other trophies of grace
In our Heavenly Home where You're making a place
And we'll see Israel crowning You, Savior, their King
Our loud "Hallelujahs!" with all we shall sing.

Eliyah (Lou) Levi was a Messianic Jew from Alexandria, Egypt, who had made *Aliyah*. I met him while volunteering at the Torch Bookshop in Yaffa Street. We married in 1982 and moved to the apartment in Narkiss street. איש of
Lou had a 'bench ministry', as he loved to strike up conversations with people. He spoke several languages. Lou passed away in 1996. We had been married 14 years.

TREE SONG

Adapted version of poem by Joyce Kilmer

I think that I shall never see
A poem lovely as a tree
A tree that looks to God all day
And lifts her leafy arms to pray.

A tree that may in **summer** wear
A nest of robins in her hair.
Against whose bosom **snow** has lain,
Who intimately lives with rain.

In **fall,** what splash of colors glow!
These glorious trees, God's 'earth-rainbow'.
He let man fell one humble tree,
On it, Christ cursed for you and me.*

* Deuteronomy 21:23; Galatians 3:13

("Poems are made by fools like me,
But only God can make a tree.") J.K.

44

BIRTHDAY POEM
Adapted

This year, dear Lord, I'm 80
And there's so much I haven't done.
I hope, dear Lord, You'll let me live
Until I'm 81.

But if I haven't finished
All that I want to do,
Would You please let me stay here
Until I'm 82?

So many places I could go,
So very much to see.
Do You think that You could manage
To make it 83?

1999 - 80th birthday celebration with friends from our Messianic Assembly

The world is changing very fast,
There's so much more in store!
I'd like it very much to live
Until I'm 84.

And if, dear Lord, by that time
I find I'm still alive,
Do You think that You could stretch it
To make it 85?

More planes will be up in the air
On earth there's much to fix.
I'll see what happens here or there
If I hit 86.

I know, dear Lord, it's much to ask,
(and It's nicer, sure, in Heaven)
But I'd really like to stay down here
Until I'm 87.

By then I'll be forgetful
Not fast, but always late.
But it would be so pleasant
To be around at 88.

I will have seen so many things;
Adventures have been mine,
So I think that I'd be willing
To leave at 89.

For all those precious years I've had,
I'm thankful, Thou Almighty,
But if it's still O.K. with You,
I'd love to live past 90.

God made my years so Heav'nly
With blessings, oh so weighty!
He said our years are 70;
By strength, He's made mine 80!*

We "fly away", verse endeth
That "Blessed Hope" ABOVE?
Though sorrows, seen or suffered,
What ever's next, Christ's LOVE.

No matter what my sum of years,
God's gift is
LIFE FOREVER.
On earth, in Heaven, with
JESUS,
Nor years, nor time, can
sever.

* Psalm 90:10

Several birthday parties have been organized by my dear friend Hela.

47

PHILISTIA vs. ZION

Thou Philistines, I hear your threat'ning
Your coat of armor looks so strong
And tho' I'm David, seen a weakling,
In Israel's God, I've "five smooth stones".

Thou whole Philistia "art dissolved"
And Zion is founded by the Lord.
Choose either your man-made 'agreement'
Or else God's true enduring Word!

Isaiah 14:31, 32

THE PALESTINE POST

CARL MARX

STATE OF ISRAEL IS BORN

The first independent Jewish State in 19 centuries was born in Tel Aviv as the British Mandate over Palestine came to an end at midnight on Friday, and it was immediately subjected to the test of fire. As "Medinat Yisrael" (State of Israel) was proclaimed, the battle for Jerusalem raged, with most of the city falling to the Jews. At the same time, President Truman announced that the United States would accord recognition to the new State. A few hours later, Palestine was invaded by Moslem armies from the south, east and north, and Tel Aviv was raided from the air. On Friday the United Nations Special Assembly adjourned after adopting a resolution to appoint a mediator but without taking any action on the Partition Resolution of November 29.

Yesterday the battle for the Jerusalem-Tel Aviv road was still under way, and two Arab villages were taken. In the north, Acre town was captured, and the Jewish Army consolidated its positions in Western Galilee.

Most Crowded Hours in Palestine's History

JEWS TAKE OVER SECURITY ZONES

Egyptian Air Force Spitfires Bomb Tel Aviv; One Shot Down

U.S. RECOGNIZES JEWISH STATE

Proclamation by Head Of Government

2 Columns Cross Southern Border

Etzion Settlers Taken P.O.W.

Special Assembly Adjourns

www.idf-armor.blogspot.com

ISRAEL'S THREE WAYS
THE FIRST WAY
Those who'd Divide the Land

We've returned to the land;
We've built it; we've planted.
We've fought wars and won,
Taking victory for granted.

But always we've known
That most Arabs hated
The sight of our coming;
Zion's dream they berated.

To rule and subdue them
Was costly, distasteful.
Though we bettered their lot,
They turned out ungrateful.

So now a new prospect
To make wars to cease:
We'll both build the land,
Each taking our piece.

We'll have our own life-style
Alongside of theirs,
In giving and taking
While all the world stares!

THE SECOND WAY
Those Against Dividing the Land

ulfilling the dream of prophets, of ours,
We've come back to Zion, turned deserts to flowers.
The nations that knew that this would transpire
Afforded us help, acclaimed our desire.

No effort was spared as we built and we ploughed,
The Scriptures our Beacon, our works spoke aloud!
The 'Ruths' who submitted to 'Naomi's' return
Found blessing with us, our gains did not spurn.

Divided before 1967,
the map looks like
two faces. Then:
Genesis 33:10; His
face - Peniel.

But now dare arise that old 'Amelek'
To thwart our revival and our building wreck?
Would he and his ilk chop up the land,
Pretending toward peace, yet a sword in his hand?

How dare we give up and dampen our zeal!
In wars brought upon us, our vict'ry we could feel.
Yet 'twas God's miracles of keeping and growth!
Now has He left us, despised us, or both?

Oh, No! We'll o'ercome no matter which way!
Our leaders may change,
But our strength we'll display.
We'll build on in faith, with Arabs make friends,
But keep the land whole, enlarged, till time ends!

50

THE THIRD WAY

Those who see it all Spiritually,
Though Possibly Combined With one of the Above

*A*braham, our father, looked for a better Land.
His faith was in the Living God Who led him by the hand.
He lived in tents, confessing, "This world is not my home",
Though dwelling as a stranger, some day no more to roam!

We who look t'ward Heaven
In Hope that far transcends,
Need never fear the wiles of man,
Their snarls, nor their trends.
We only need to turn **their** hearts
Also unto the Lord,
Who gives us Life eternal, His Love,
His Living Word.

Then where we are, one Family,
In mutual love and care.
Concerns of worldly powers,
We'll let our Father bear!
He's Prince of Peace, earth's Sacrifice,
The Way to what we want,
In 'Tents of Shem', Truth's pure **root** shared:
Semitic Treasure hunt!

51

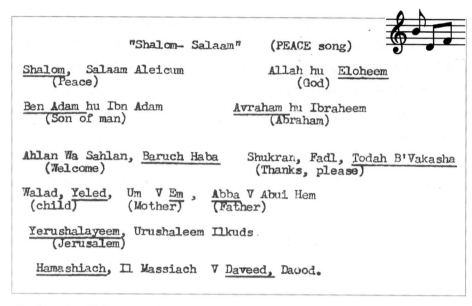

"Shalom– Salaam"   (PEACE song)

Shalom,   Salaam Aleicum   Allah hu   Eloheem
    (Peace)   (God)

Ben Adam hu Ibn Adam   Avraham hu Ibraheem
   (Son of man)   (Abraham)

Ahlan Wa Sahlan, Baruch Haba   Shukran, Fadl, Todah B'Vakasha
   (Welcome)   (Thanks, please)

Walad, Yeled,   Um V Em ,   Abba V Abui Hem
  (child)   (Mother)   (Father)

Yerushalayeem, Urushaleem Ilkuds
   (Jerusalem)

Hamashiach, Il Massiach V Daveed, Daood.

Explanation Hebrew underlined words: V - 'and' ; Hem - 'they' ; Hu - 'is'

THE STORY BEHIND THE SONG

In 1972, Anita Kiekhaefer, an experienced film maker from America, and I wrote the script for a film about Jewish-Arab relations. The 30 minute production was called *"Shalom-Salaam"*. (See *From McComb to Jerusalem* page 149 v.v.).

On July 30, 1980, the Jerusalem Law passed in the Knesset (Israel's parliament). The city of Jerusalem was to be the undivided, eternal capital of the State of Israel, established as such by King David, almost 3,000 years ago. Teddy Kollek had become the mayor of all Jerusalem - East and West. "Maybe, if we made a song about peace, we'll get peace," Kollek said in a radio broadcast. His words inspired me to write the song "Shalom-Salaam", which I recorded on tape and gave it to Teddy Kollek. He was very pleased. (See *From McComb to Jerusalem* page 185).

52

SEMITIC BLESSINGS
TO THE WORLD

Dedicated to Richard and Sabina Wurmbrand on their trips to Israel.
They suffered greatly from the hands of the Nazis and Communists. Richard spoke fourteen languages! Root words, in many meanings
in Hebrew and Arabic, are here put into English.

My friendship with the Wurmbrands lasted a lifetime.

T he world must know, the universe, mankind,
That Invisible revealed, through the virgin, His sign;
The name manifest through Shem and his seed,
And Semitic Scripture - "tents of Shem" indeed!

God's peace has been made through that Peace-offering.
We're complete, since He paid! Made perfect, we sing!
He was yielded to death, that we might have life.
We surrender to Him, climb peace ladder, end strife.

We're loosed from the curse! It's finished! Salvation!
Made pure and restored; loins girt against Satan.
We'll overcome, be sincere, in true faith through One ~
Our Counselor, Victor, Eternal, Chief Musician.

How lovely! What delight! So commendable, praise!
Praise to God beautifies even unlovely days.
To rejoice, to be happy, is to blossom - a flower.
It's to fly and to flourish; joy and beauty each hour.

The One, our Head-Stone, both Father and Son,
Is building His Temple of sons, 'living stones'.
In us He abides, "*Shekinah*" and we're calmed
Where we dwell, with our neighbors.
We're His '*Mishkan*'.

Look up, all ye rescued, redemption draws nigh;
The Bright Morning star in the
eastern sky,
Will appear in full glory.
See Him even now shine:
Star of David, of Bethlehem,
Shield, Thou art mine.

Visiting my friends while in the States.

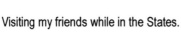

ARE *THESE* JEWS FOOLS?

**Dedicated to
Jewish believers
in Jesus (*Yeshua*),
~~Christ~~ the Messiah
~~In Greek~~ etc.**

Shavuot 1967 - Jewish believers were finally able to visit the Garden Tomb in East Jerusalem, which until the 6 Day War, had been occupied by Jordan.

[handwritten annotations: "Garden Tomb" "All in Yeshua" "Jesus who believe in Yeshua"]

*C*ome now, and let us reason together.
Would one be so foolish (Not tell me whether)
As to fervently say that he holds dear
One whom his friends all hate or fear,
If Christ were not true?

Who wants to be hated, despised, cast off,
Called *"meshummad"* (or traitor) by those who scoff,
(As though he'd betrayed his father and mother,
And left Israel's God, to follow another)
If Christ were not true?

What gain would there be in losing all -
Your job or your home - just to heed a call,
Changing from sin to a life of glory
With one great aim - just to share His story,
If Christ were not true?

Would Abraham, David, Solomon, all bother
Those thousands of sacrifice lambs to slaughter,
And God's prophets tell - the Anointed would come,
Keeping God's law, by **His** death, save **us** from,
If Christ were not true?

Why would those Jewish shepherds that night,
Led by God's Word and the angel sight,
Forsake their sheep for Bethlehem's manger
There to worship a Babe and a Stranger
If Christ were not true?

Christ's twelve disciples, and more Jews as well,
In Jesus saw their Emmanuel.
Would they at His death, so filled with fear once
Now be bold as lions through His appearance
If Christ were not true?

Certainly Paul, who hated and chased,
His fellow-Jews who owned Jesus Christ,
Would not turn to preach this Same One, seen from Heaven,
Off among Gentiles and Jews - his loved brethren;
If Christ were not true?

Were Christ just a teacher, prophet, good man -
Along with many hundreds of them,
Then why would these lay down their lives, I ask,
To preach Him, a thankless and un-needed task,
If Christ were not true?

Not true when He said, "I'll make you free";
"None comes to the Father excepting by Me"?
How He healed, helped and taught, later rising again,
After laying down that Jewish life for our sin.
You say Christ's not true?

Then where will you flee when God's judgments fall
Upon the wrong doers, and that includes all?
How can you know God's deep peace within
When He's hid His face from you, thru' your much sin,
If Christ is not true?

Ah, friend, He is true! That's why these Jews dare
To live for Him, die for Him, here, everywhere!
He is the Messiah! They've found Him! Have you?
You'll see how they couldn't help tell it - it's true
When YOU see Christ's love too!

But if, without reason, you say, "Yes, they're fools!"
They're out of their minds when they break all our rules.
Whether God or the angels, the Bible, or reason
Changed them to follow this Jesus - it's treason!
You'll NOT want the Truth.

In this way you show that God's Word is true.
He plainly has shown there a picture of you:
The 'cross' is but 'foolish' to those that perish,
God's wisdom, salvation, to those who cherish
Messiah, Who's **so** true!

TWO JERUSALEMS

(sung as a round)

Millennial Jerusalem

Jerusalem, City of peace
Jesus shall reign here
And wars all shall cease
Thou, this world's Light,
Make all things right
Come to Jerusalem.

Messiah will enter Jerusalem
through the Golden Gate

Heavenly Jerusalem

God's new Jerusalem
Out of Heaven she'll come
Bride of the Savior Lamb
We're that Jerusalem.

(These two songs can be sung together as a round.)

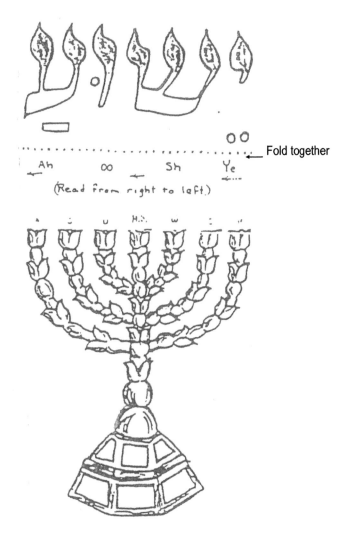

Fold together

Ah   ∞   —   Sh   Ye

(Read from right to left.)

I always carry copies of this card in my purse, and whenever I can, I show people that *YESHUA* is the Light of Israel.